WHEN THE BORDERS BLEED

WHEN THE BORDERS BLEED

THE STRUGGLE OF THE KURDS

Photographs by Ed Kashi

Introduction by Christopher Hitchens

Pantheon Books   New York

Library of Congress Cataloging-in-Publication Data

Kashi, Ed.
When the borders bleed : the struggle of the Kurds /
photographs by Ed Kashi ; introduction by Christopher
Hitchens.
p.   cm.
Includes bibliographical references.
ISBN 0-679-43337-6
1. Kurds—Politics and government.   2. Middle East—Politics and
government—1945–   I. Title.
DS59.K86K34   1994
956´.0049159—dc20   93–50156

Book design by Fearn Cutler

Map by Joan Kristensen / Siren Design

Manufactured in the United States of America
First Edition
9 8 7 6 5 4 3 2 1

Borders are scratched across the hearts of men

By strangers with a calm, judicial pen,

And when the borders bleed we watch with dread

The lines of ink along the map turn red.

—Marya Mannes

A brave man dies once; a timid man dies daily.

—Kurdish proverb

◧ CONTENTS

❈ PREFACE

My first encounter with Kurdistan actually took place in Northern Ireland, where, in early 1990, I met a British artist and his Kurdish wife. During the next year I spent many nights in their east London flat discussing the Kurdish people, their ancient culture, and their contemporary fight for survival, as well as the atrocities committed against them, most of which have gone unreported by the Western press. Before ever setting foot in Kurdistan, I became obsessed with the Kurds, their plight, and their futile attempts to secure a homeland.

The Kurds are the largest ethnic group in the world without a nation, numbering over twenty million people with a common language and culture. Kurdish history came to a virtual standstill after World War I, when the region known as Kurdistan was divided between five newly formed nations: Iran, Iraq, Turkey, Syria, and the former Soviet Republic of Armenia. This partitioning by the League of Nations obliterated thousands of years of Kurdish claims to the region and set in motion decades of oppression, culminating in the ruthless chemical warfare waged against them by the Iraqi government, whose troops leveled more than four thousand Iraqi Kurdish towns and villages over the last two decades.

Toward the end of 1990 I started to plan my first trip to Kurdistan, which would begin in the ancient city of Diyarbakir, Turkey. But by then Iraqi troops had occupied Kuwait, and the United States and its allies were poised to erupt into Operation Desert Storm. My project to document the Kurds was in danger of being overshadowed by the Gulf War. Little did I know that the Kurds would dominate front-page headlines in the coming months.

The ground war ended by late February 1991, and Operation Provide Comfort began its effort to rescue nearly a million Iraqi Kurdish refugees stranded in the mountains between Iraq and Turkey. I wrote to Tom Kennedy, the director of photography at *National Geographic* magazine, suggesting that the *Geographic* underwrite my efforts to document the life and struggle of the Kurds. We had never worked together, but with a great leap of faith he stood behind me and assigned the widely acclaimed political writer Christopher Hitchens to the story.

By late April 1991 I was off to Diyarbakir, but the scope of the story had expanded way beyond Turkey. I now had the means to cover six countries over a six-month shooting schedule. In addition to the ancient alleyways of Diyarbakir, I scoured the refugee camps in Turkey and Iran, and I witnessed firsthand the landscape of destruction left behind by Iraqi troops. In Lebanon's infamous Bekaa Valley, I visited the training camp for the Kurdistan Workers Party (PKK), an armed Kurdish separatist movement fighting in southeastern Turkey, and I managed to move in and out of Iran under the ever-watchful eyes of the secret police. I froze through a fierce winter with young Kurdish gangs in the streets of Berlin and with courageous refugees living without heat or electricity in the rubble in northern Iraq. On Christmas Day, 1991, I returned to Washington, D.C., from the last of three trips, having shot more than 1,100 rolls of film.

As I write this, the Kurdish situation remains dire at best: in Turkey, the government's denial of past injustices and its continued repression constitute a state of siege in the Kurdish region. This, combined with the armed movement of the PKK, has resulted in more than seven thousand deaths since 1984. In the past two years alone, more than sixteen journalists have been killed in the area.

In Iraq, for the first time in modern history, the Kurds are autonomous, but tens of thousands of Iraqi troops amassed along the border of sovereign Kurdistan threaten this foundling nation's security. In the meantime, the Kurds struggle to endure the food and fuel embargo imposed by Baghdad, and Saddam's agents continue to terrorize UN relief workers and destroy supply vehicles bound for Kurdistan.

Although little is ever heard about the plight of the Kurds in Iran, their oppression continues. In 1993, three of the most powerful Iranian Kurdish leaders were gunned down in a Berlin restaurant during a meeting. In Syria, under the heavy-handed rule of Hafez al-Assad, the Kurds are effectively muted by their small numbers and their inability to organize a strong opposition.

For a brief moment after the Gulf War, the Kurdish story commanded world attention, but it has since been relegated to the back page. In an age of disposable news, the Kurds are in danger of being quickly forgotten, even though their suffering continues with no end in sight. From the genocidal campaign in Iraq to the insidious oppression in Turkey, the Kurds fight daily to maintain their lives, their land, and their language. For anyone who comes in contact with the Kurds, it is impossible to remain silent. This book is a tribute to the strength and dignity of the Kurdish people.

Ed Kashi
San Francisco, 1993

❈ ACKNOWLEDGMENTS

This collection of photographs would not have been possible without the cooperation of the Kurdish people. I was continually amazed by the Kurds' spirit, strength, and grace in the face of the most punishing conditions I have ever experienced. I would like to thank so many of them personally, but for their own safety I cannot name names. I am forever indebted to one Kurdish man from Diyarbakir who worked with me as a guide and interpreter through much of the project, traveling with me illegally in Iraq and at great personal risk in Turkey, where he could have disappeared all too easily without a word. I worry for his continued safety in light of the many assassinations of Kurdish journalists in the region. In November of 1992 he was wounded by Turkish security forces.

Thanks to Stuart and Maya Brisley, my friends in London who got me interested in this subject, and to Maya in particular for her insights and for writing the chronology for this book. To Rich Amdur, my dear friend, who helped me write that first letter to the *Geographic*. To Linda Asher, who stuck through thick and thin with me and my work for nine years, and who helped me put together the proposal for this project. To Jane Palecek for her patience, support, and wisdom during the grueling year I was working on this story.

Thanks to Christopher Hitchens for adding a different dimension to my work and life; Joan Kristensen for her beautiful work on the map for this book; Vera Beaudin Saeedpour for her incredible support and devotion to the Kurdish cause; Estella Schmid for her courage, commitment, and zeal; and the Kurdish centers in London, Berlin, and Cologne for their invaluable assistance. Love and thanks to Julie Winokur for donning the editor's cap to refine the words and images for this book.

I also want to thank the people at *National Geographic*, especially Tom Kennedy, Kent Kobersteen, Susan Welchman, Heidi Ernst, Dave Griffin, Erla Zwingle, Bill Allen, Bob Poole, and Bill Graves.

Finally, I want to thank my Baghdad-born mother and father, who were always on my mind while I was in Iraq.

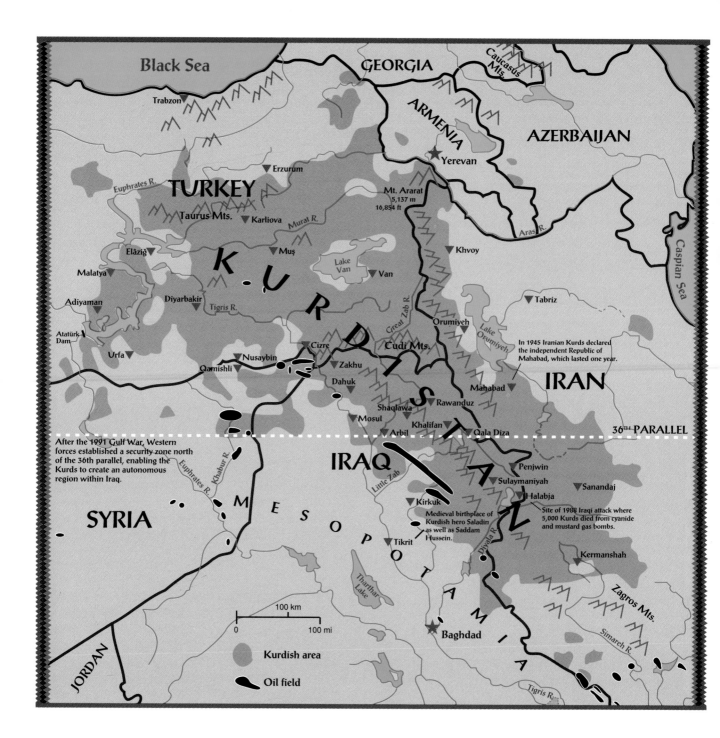

Black Sea

GEORGIA

Caucasus Mts.

ARMENIA

AZERBAIJAN

Trabzon

Erzurum

TURKEY

Euphrates R.

Taurus Mts.

Karliova

Murat R.

Mt. Ararat
5,137 m
16,854 ft

Yerevan

K U R D Elâziğ

Muş

Malatya

Lake
Van

Van

Khvoy

Aras R.

Caspian Sea

Adiyaman

Diyarbakir

Tigris R.

Tabriz

Atatürk
Dam

Urfa

Nusaybin

Cizre

Cudi Mts.

Great Zab R.

Orumiyeh

Lake
Orumiyeh

In 1945 Iranian Kurds declared
the independent Republic of
Mahabad, which lasted one year.

Qamishli

Zakhu

Dahuk

Mahabad

IRAN

Shaqlawa

Rawanduz

Mosul

Khalifan

Qala Diza

36ᵀᴴ PARALLEL

Arbil

After the 1991 Gulf War, Western
forces established a security zone north
of the 36th parallel, enabling the
Kurds to create an autonomous
region within Iraq.

IRAQ

Penjwin

Sulaymaniyah

Sanandaj

Khabur R.

Euphrates R.

M E S O P O T A M I A

Little Zab

Kirkuk

Halabja

Site of 1988 Iraqi attack where
5,000 Kurds died from cyanide
and mustard gas bombs.

SYRIA

Medieval birthplace of
Kurdish hero Saladin
as well as Saddam
Hussein.

Diyala R.

Kermanshah

Tikrit

Tharthar
Lake

Zagros Mts.

100 km

0   100 mi

Kurdish area

Oil field

Baghdad

Simareh R.

Tigris R.

JORDAN

▨ INTRODUCTION

by Christopher Hitchens

A general in the Iraqi army, a veteran of the Gulf War, wakes one morning in Baghdad and decides to take a few trusted men into the northern mountains, resolved never to return.

A waiter in an Armenian restaurant in Aleppo, Syria, upon learning that I visited a certain training camp in Lebanon's Bekaa Valley, puts down his tray and, to the puzzlement of onlookers, raises a fist in the air and says "PKK!"

A woman social worker in the Spandau district of Berlin faces another day of neo-Nazi graffiti at her place of work and lobbies the local school for classes in a strange, ancient language.

In a house in Nicosia, Cyprus, a poet who works for the Palestine Liberation Organization hears of a chemical warfare massacre in a country he has never seen and writes a long verse tribute. The poem is called *Mahabad*—the name of a city he has never visited, but a name with nearly magical power for the few who understand it.

In an elegant restaurant in Jerusalem, a senior member of the municipal government dines with friends. They talk excitedly, lovingly, of a far-off place their fathers knew and had left, never to return.

In southeastern Turkey, a philosophy student interrupts a discussion of Greek ideas to fiddle with a radio dial. He picks up a station in the former Soviet Caucasus, broadcasting in a tongue which may not be spoken on local airwaves.

In San Diego, California, a computer technician takes time off from his work to help produce a cultural and political magazine named *Halabja*, for a town gutted of its people in an Iraqi gas attack.

All of these people—General Mufti, Jamal the waiter, Aso Agace the social worker, Salim Barakat the poet, Aharon Sarig the Israeli official, Ibrahim Çalan the philosophy student, and Alan Zangana the computer operator—are Kurds. Along with their arduous and unique history, they all became the unexpected responsibility of the world in early 1991. The Kurds were as startled to be discovered as was the West to discover them. The history of Kurdish life and culture, however, is a litany of sudden shifts, as well as of betrayals and abandonments.

Who are these people, and where do they come from? Anthropology and ethnology tell us that they are Indo-European or Aryan, a finding more intriguing than definitive. It is easier to state what they are not: not Arab, not Persian, not Turkish. Travelers to the region which these people have occupied for more than two thousand years have been reporting for centuries on the blue or green eyes, the fair hair and complexions of the Kurds, but shade and coloring do not a nation make. If we take Winston Churchill's famous remark that "a man is of the race which he passionately believes himself to be," we are on safer ground.

Around 400 B.C., as the Greeks were retreating

toward the Black Sea, Xenophon recorded that they were harassed along the way by Karduchoi —evidently a fierce, martial people. Fifteen centuries later, as the Muslim world strove to expel the Crusaders, it was the Kurdish warrior Salah al-Din, better known to posterity as Saladin, who conquered Jerusalem (he was also the military governor of the Mesopotamian town of Tikrit—later the birthplace of Saddam Hussein).

Throughout the intervening and later centuries, the Kurds lived like other large minorities, by sniffing the wind and being tactically adroit. Claiming descent from the semimythical Medes, they professed the Sunni Islam of the majority of their neighbors while sheltering in their ranks the adherents of every conceivable sect and faith. Their language, at once highly distinctive and much fragmented by dialect, has been passed on orally; it has also survived in Aramaic, Arabic, Persian, and Turkish written texts. A stable and continuous element in the Mesopotamia/Anatolia/Caucasia region, the Kurds were dragged into modern history with the rise of empires and nation-states, which took upon themselves the task of deciding who the Kurds were and how their fate should be determined for them.

The Kurds number perhaps twenty million people, which makes them the largest national group in the world without a state of their own. They are cursed by living in a landlocked area rich in oil, which adjoins the territory of many warring and suspicious rivals; where the borders of Iran, Iraq, Syria, and Turkey converge. Arabs and Per-

sians, Turks and Arabs, Armenians and Turks, Russians and Turks—these are animosities that extend back for centuries, and when they erupt into conflict the Kurds are often trapped in the middle.

The historical memory of the Kurds is one of endlessly cheated aspirations. Their past and their location have combined to make them the classic victims of geopolitics. An experienced Kurd can tell his grandchildren of betrayal by colonial Britain and France; of promises made by Iran, Iraq, and Turkey to sustain the Kurds only for as long as they were fighting on a rival's territory; of ostensibly friendly interventions in Kurdistan by Israel which were really intended to divide and weaken Arab regimes; of pacts broken by Arab nationalists in the name of solidarity with Palestine; and of undertakings made by both Cold War superpowers that turned out to be false.

In 1918, shocked and embarrassed by the Bolshevik disclosure of a planned Anglo-French carve-up of the post–World War I Middle East, President Woodrow Wilson issued his Fourteen Points. The twelfth of these stated that the non-Turkish peoples in the Ottoman sphere, such as the Kurds and the Armenians, should be "assured of an absolute unmolested opportunity of autonomous development." When the victorious Allies met to sign the Treaty of Sèvres in August 1920, they gave expression to Wilsonian principles by declaring that an Allied commission would

prepare for local autonomy in those regions where the Kurdish element is preponderant, lying east of the

Euphrates, to the south of the still-to-be-established Armenian frontier and to the north of the frontier between Turkey, Syria, and Mesopotamia.

This initiative did not come without conditions, not least because the British—especially Winston Churchill—coveted the northern Iraqi oilfields.

During the post-1918 British mandate over what was then Mesopotamia—"the land between the rivers"—Churchill, then the colonial secretary, strove to pacify Iraq with the newest military technology, air power. Among the indigenous population the Kurds proved the hardest to subdue. The Kurdish village of Barzan in northern Iraq became one of the first places ever to be destroyed from the sky by the British Royal Air Force. Churchill's goal was to create a single, centralized, pro-British state that would command the oilfields of Kirkuk and Mosul. His method of colonizing Iraq anticipated the even more pitiless version of "nation-building" that Iraqi nationalists would later practice.

In the Treaty of Sèvres, the Kurds were asked to demonstrate that they were "capable of . . . independence." But despite the conditions, the Kurds regarded the treaty as a formal international acknowledgment of their rights (by, among others, Turkey, which was a signatory to the treaty). The "window of opportunity," however, lasted hardly any longer than subsequent ones. The Turkish government was overthrown by General Mustafa Kemal, later known as Atatürk, who resented the attempted dismemberment of the Turkish heart-land. Ottoman rule was replaced by a strongly military and nationalist leadership, which repelled an invading Greek army, expelled surviving Greeks and Armenians from Anatolia, and forced a renegotiation of the treaty. As rewritten at Lausanne in 1923, the new treaty excluded any mention of the Kurds, let alone of their rights to self-determination. For the next few decades, all expressions of Kurdish nationalism were put down with extreme thoroughness, and the official dogma of the Kurds as "mountain Turks" was imposed.

Mahabad is a town in northern Iran that was, for a brief period after World War II, the capital of an autonomous state. Taking advantage of an early Cold War tussle between the Anglo-American and Soviet forces in what was then Persia, the Kurdish leadership established its first and only foothold on sovereign soil. As East and West squabbled over the oilfields and future of the Shah, the Republic of Mahabad was proclaimed on New Year's Day, 1946. Its president was Qazi Muhammed, a local notable who was popular enough to reconcile differences between old-style nationalists and pro-Moscow communists.

For a while, the infant republic looked as if it might be able to survive and provide an example to Kurds in other countries. A large stroke of good fortune for the Mahabadis came when Mullah Mustafa Barzani, the legendary leader of the Kurdish insurgency in Iraq, arrived with a small army of hard-core followers. He was conducting one of his many strategic retreats, this time from the British-installed Hashemite monarchy then ruling in Baghdad. Meanwhile, Mahabad became a center for the publication of Kurdish books and periodicals, and also some rather clumsy attempts at land redistribution.

But the republic suffered chronically from two disadvantages: the small size of its territory; and the fratricidal and tribal nature of Kurdish life in Iran. Many local chieftains saw in Mahabad's leadership a challenge to their own authority, while others had a deep-rooted dislike of the Soviet influence. The latter was ironic, for the Soviet Union under Stalin was actually not at all disposed to put itself out for the Kurdish experiment.

By the middle of 1946, the Red Army had been evacuated from Iran, and Moscow confined itself to a few rhetorical gestures of support for Qazi Muhammed. Seeking to restore its bruised authority after so many years of Allied occupation, the central government in Tehran moved an army northward in December 1946. Many Kurds waited to see who would win, and some threw in their lot with the government; Mahabad fell without much resistance. The "Republic" had lasted less than one year.

Barzani and his men moved back across the Iraqi border and thence to the Soviet Union, where he was to stay under Red Army protection for several years. Qazi Muhammed chose to stay, and surrendered. Despite the intervention of the American diplomat Archie Roosevelt, who pleaded with the Shah's regime to spare him, Muhammed was hanged in the main square of Mahabad in March 1947. The Kurdish presses and publishing houses were destroyed, and the teaching of the Kurdish language was once again prohibited. Although the name of Mahabad came to evoke a bygone moment of independence, with the hope (or promise) of its return, the Soviet Union could be added to the long list of nations that had betrayed the Kurds in a crisis.

Subsequent instances of the victimization of the Kurds principally involved the United States. Prior to 1975, the Kurdish rebels commanded by Mullah Mustafa Barzani had improved their position in northern Iraq, thanks in large part to arms, aid, and training from Iran, Israel, and the United States. Under the Nixon-Kissinger doctrine, American aid to the Kurds served as a favor to the Shah and a warning to Arab nationalists. But in March 1975, the Shah of Iran met Saddam Hussein at an OPEC summit in Algiers and publicly shook hands on an agreement over the Shatt al-Arab waterway—the original cause of the dispute between the two nations and the reason for the Shah's destabilization campaign against Baghdad in the first place.

Iraq's price for the deal was not especially high. It had made concessions in the south. In return, Iran was to cut off the supply line to Barzani, with immediate effect. The U. S. House Select Committee on Intelligence later found that

the Kurds were clearly taken by surprise as well, while the Iraqis, knowing of the impending aid cut-off, launched an all-out search-and-destroy campaign the day after the agreement was signed. The autonomy movement was over. . . .

Casualty estimates were in the thousands; in addition, 200,000 people became refugees.

As more evidence became available, it became apparent that the conception of the covert operation in Kurdistan had been as crudely exploitative as its terminus proved to be. The House committee established that

the President, Dr. Kissinger and the Shah hoped that our clients would not prevail. They preferred instead that the insurgents simply continue a level of hostilities sufficient to sap the resources of our ally's neighboring country. This policy was not imparted to our clients, who were encouraged to continue fighting. Even in the context of covert operations, ours was a cynical enterprise.

The search-and-destroy campaign in Iraqi Kurdistan continued through the Iran-Iraq war and beyond. In Kurdistan, the word *anfal* is often spoken in distraught tones. *Anfal* is a Koranic concept, supposedly based on a verse in the Holy Book exhorting the Prophet and believers to give no quarter to enemies and nonbelievers. Ali Hassan al-Majid, the Iraqi defense minister, baptized his 1988 campaign in Kurdistan "Operation Anfal" and the term stuck. (Mr. al-Majid went on to supervise the Kuwait annexation, drawing heavily on tactics rehearsed in the Anfal campaign.)

By 1988, researchers and staffers from the U.S. Senate Committee on Foreign Relations were convinced that Iraq's armed forces were waging a coordinated campaign of atrocities against the Kurds. On the basis of their finding, Senator Claiborne Pell, the committee chairman, introduced the Prevention of Genocide Act. At the time, however, Washington-Baghdad relations were warm, and White House clout was exerted to drop the bill before it could become law. Official doctrine under Ronald Reagan, and then George Bush, mandated a tilt toward Iraq as a regional ally and trading partner. At the height of the Anfal campaign, the United States was sharing intelligence with Iraq and ignoring or contesting *prima facie* evidence of genocide gathered by some of its own diplomats.

During the Gulf War, Turkey became an important member of the Western coalition against Iraq. More than any issue save that of Kuwait, it had been Saddam Hussein's treatment of the Kurds that made him an international pariah. But on the Kurdish question, Iraq and Turkey seemed to have an unspoken agreement. At the beginning of 1991, Kurdish refugees flooded out of Iraq and into Turkey. The Turkish government put out a lavish brochure in several languages proclaiming its humane response to what it called "Northern Iraqis."

By the middle of 1991, Turkish planes and troops were striking northern Iraq to eliminate the bases of Kurdish guerrillas. By then, the attention of the world was elsewhere. As Jalal Talabani, leader of the Patriotic Union of Kurdistan, told me: "The West only liberated Kuwait and nothing else." His ally Sami Abdul Raman, leader of the Kurdish Peoples Democratic Party and, before his defection, former Iraqi cabinet minister for Kurdish affairs, was even pithier: "When the Americans came they didn't ask us; when they left they didn't tell us. I hope that the great love for the United States among my people is justified." On the hood of the jeep that drove me through Kurdistan was taped a color photograph of George Bush, jogging. It would not be there today—and not simply for aesthetic reasons. Even in a history very rich in betrayal, American duplicity stands as something of a benchmark.

Though the Gulf War occasioned yet another betrayal of the Kurds, it also resulted in a partial vindication of their cause. As the coalition against Iraq accomplished its military objective of freeing Kuwait, CIA radio stations based in Saudi Arabia broadcast appeals for an uprising against Saddam Hussein's government. More of a promise than a suggestion of American help in the effort was given. The Kurdish population responded eagerly, but when it saw that Iraq's helicopter gunships were still flying and Hussein's Republican Guard was still intact, mass flight ensued. The images of exodus and terror were so potent on Western television screens that an improvised policy of aid and protection was hastily put into effect by the British, French, and United States governments. A makeshift autonomy was created by a network of "safe havens." Refugees who had fled to Iran and Turkey began to return. The Kurdish militias began to regroup. Informal border posts began to spring up near towns like Kirkuk and Sulaymaniyah, which the Kurds had taken during the uprising but had later lost.

The latest ad hoc efforts of the West notwithstanding, it has seemed that, no matter what they do or which allies they make, the Kurds can only be safe in what Carleton Coon, in his famous book *Caravan*, called "the Land of Insolence": that is, the reliance of the Kurd on his own right arm and the weapon in his belt, and his faith in the power of the stubborn mountains and gorges of Kurdistan to wear down any foe. A popular Kurdish saying expresses this almost desperate self-reliance: "The Kurds have no friends—no friends but the mountains."

I had a chance to consider this long and melancholy story in July 1991, while sitting in a broken-down car in the village of Barzan. It was evening, and a U.S. Air Force jet was arrowing loftily down the valley of the River Zab, as if to bring on the sunset. The whole area was deserted and still, even though it had recently been home to several thousand mountain-dwelling Kurds. Barzan was like dozens of other villages I had seen: a destroyed stone hamlet with vegetation sprouting over the rough outlines of ruin. But since this had been the home of the renowned Barzani clan, it could be taken as an emblem of sorts of desolate Iraqi Kurdistan.

The local Kurds had gone where they always go in time of trouble—deep into the hills. Unlike in the past, however, they had been able to leave many of their children and women in refugee camps at various frontiers. The towns of Zakho and Dahuk, through which my party had passed, were the latest headline-makers in the history of international disaster relief. But the lure of the mountains had drawn some civilians too. The heart of Kurdistan is the mountain territory where the borders of the four neighbors converge, and when I saw it this heart was in the process of being torn out.

The road south of Shaqlawa, the hill town that acts as the headquarters of the numerous Kurdish guerrilla groups, passes through a series of demolished villages and leads to Qala Diza, a town near the Iranian border. In June 1989, Iraqi demolition and punishment squads were sent there to make an example of the place. With bulldozers and dynamite they leveled the entire town. Our guide, Hoshyar Samsam, the personal bodyguard to Jalal Talabani, took us to the one surviving clinic. There, Dr. Osman Salim dispensed medicine as best he could from his small stock. The problems he faced were the familiar Third World trio of malnutrition, typhoid, and malaria, all exacerbating each other's effects. Those who could not or would not flee were living in the ruins, with unclean water and poor food, and not enough of either. Dr. Salim was surprised to hear that the Kurdish people had become a humanitarian issue in the Western media. You could not tell that by any shipment that had come his way, he said. And what was to happen when winter arrived? Meanwhile, old people showed us dog-eared photographs of how their town once looked.

We quit Qala Diza and pushed on down arduous roads toward Halabja. Everywhere we saw armed Kurdish guerrilla fighters, known as the Pesh Merga—literally, "those who face death." For Kurdish males, childhood means familiarity with weapons, and most of the men we met would have

seemed—and no doubt felt—naked without a gun. This is real border country, with a long intransigent tradition. But in recent years, these toughened guerrillas have had to face weapons they couldn't even see. Thus we were making for Halabja and skirting a detour around Iraqi lines.

Halabja is to the Kurds what the Warsaw ghetto is to the Jews, or Guernica to the Basques, or Wounded Knee to the Sioux. On March 16, 1988, Amina Mohammed Amin, a school custodian in her early fifties, saw the planes come, the bombs fall and explode. Living as she did in a combat zone, she was relatively inured to warfare. But she knew at once that something unprecedented was happening. Riding on a tractor making its way out of town, she felt a sudden burning sensation on her skin and in her eyes, and only later noticed that her hair and eyebrows had been scorched also. Her skin is still seared by burns that don't heal. Twenty-five of her relatives perished in the attack; they were among the nearly five thousand citizens who died never knowing what hit them.

Those responsible for the attack tried to hide it amid the confusion of war, but hard evidence exists. In the basement of a nearby ruined house, I found the embedded shell of an unexploded chemical bomb with the markings of the Iraqi air force. Iraqi soldiers had entered the poisoned community and taken away all the unexploded canisters they could find, but did a hasty, sloppy job. Despite their efforts, Halabja will be remembered.

As will much else. Like this story told me by Siamand Banaa, a spokesman for the Kurdish Democratic Party: "We had almost eight thousand males above the age of twelve removed by the government from the region of Barzan village and placed in a 'relocation center.' In 1983, when the war with Iran was going badly, these men and boys were taken to Baghdad and paraded as 'prisoners of war' on August 3. We could see them on TV. Since then, nothing has been heard of them. You get rumors, of course—that they were used as compulsory blood donors for the troops at the front, or as guinea pigs for the chemical warfare program, or as target practice. . . ."

As I made my way back overland from Iraq, I arrived in the Turkish city of Diyarbakir, a handsome, ancient town surrounded by walls of basalt, and found it under martial law. The predominantly Kurdish population was seething at the murder of one of its leaders, Mr. Vedat Aydin of the Peoples Labor Party (HEP), who had been slain death-squad style. At his funeral, several members of parliament had been beaten unconscious by the police and the large crowd of mourners had been fired upon. Accounts of the riot varied, as did reports of the cause and of the number of casualties—the inevitable result of censorship. Surly Turkish soldiers kept me off the road to the village of Nusaybin, where there was said to be more unrest.

In Diyarbakir itself, elevator boys and waiters would whisper to Westerners such as myself: "We are not Turks . . . this is not Turkey . . . we are Kurds . . . this is Kurdistan." After quite a tussle, I managed to board a plane to Ankara with five or six heavily bandaged parliamentarians, who were flying back to the capital with more fruitless complaints about the situation in a province where the Kurdish flag is prohibited and the Kurdish language, for most public purposes, banned.

Harold Pinter depicts Turkey's oppressive policies toward the Kurds in his one-act play *Mountain Language*, written in protest after a trip to that country. An officer says to a group of women gathered outside a prison:

Now hear this. You are mountain people. You hear me? Your language is dead. It is forbidden. It is not permitted to speak your mountain language in this place. You cannot speak your language to your men. It is not permitted. You may not speak it. It is outlawed. You may only speak the language of the capital. . . .

Yet, discussion of the Kurdish "problem," long taboo in the Turkish media, has become more bold and open since Desert Storm and the publicity given to the Kurds in Iraq. During my stay, a column by Hasan Çemal was published in the respected Turkish daily *Cumhuriyet* (Republic). He recalled his military service at the American base in Boztepe, near Trabzon:

Most of the soldiers under my command were of Kurdish descent. One of the soldiers, who had the same name as myself, Sergeant Haso, had a strange habit. He used to come to me every evening at the same time to borrow my transistor radio. I became curious and, after one of his visits, decided to follow him.

I wasn't noticed as I walked into the dormitory. They were all preoccupied listening to the doleful music coming from the radio. After a short while they noticed my presence, and came to attention as if coming out of a trance. The song was not Turkish, so I asked them which radio station they were listening to. Nervously and guiltily, like a child reprimanded for doing something terribly wrong, Sergeant Haso stepped forward and said "Iran." There were Kurdish songs being transmitted from the Kurdish service of Radio Iran. . . .

Anyone who spends any time with Kurds knows the importance they attach to folk music, and the trouble they will go to in order to find cassettes or tune into obscure radio stations to hear the songs of such musicians as Juwan Hajo, a Syrian Kurd from Qamishli, whose tapes are bootlegged all over the region; or Shivan Perwer from Diyarbakir, a favorite among Kurds in Turkey and Germany. Given the extent of illiteracy and the survival of Kurdish primarily in oral rather than written form, the power of music and folksong is hard to overstate.

In his column, Çemal went on to discuss the abduction and murder of Vedat Aydin in Diyarbakir and compared it to "the Latin American system." It may well be that the greatest unintended consequence of Desert Storm will be the rekindling of Kurdish nationalism in a NATO country. Although the late Prime Minister Turgut Ozal made some suggestive concessions on the principle of Kurdish nationhood (even admitting in public to some Kurdish ancestry of his own), the tempo of the war in the Kurdish provinces has risen, along with expectations.

Like all oppressed and disregarded nations, the Kurds have a tendency to blame all their woes on foreign interlopers, but they will also often admit privately that, left to themselves, they become fractious. I went to Lebanon to meet Abdullah Öçalan, known as Apo ("uncle") to his followers and Sarouk ("leader") to his hard-core enthusiasts. Öçalan is perhaps the sternest critic of the Kurds' own traditions; he regards their leaders as backward and feudal.

Beirut airport is a harrowing place to be on one's own. A succession of intermediaries had promised me that my flight would be met by members of the PKK. It wasn't, and I had a few sticky moments in the darkened, battered, chaotic terminal when unshaven, smoking Lebanese gendarmes asked whom I was waiting for. (One of them later offered to act as my taxi driver for American dollars.) The next day the PKK contacted me at my hotel. They had been at the airport, they said, but had been afraid to approach when they saw me talking to the police.

The life of the Lebanese Kurds is one of constant avoidance of authority. The state is notoriously organized along religious lines, with reserved places for Maronite Christians, Druzes, Sunni and Shi'a Muslims, and smaller denominations. But there is no clear citizenship for national minorities and a distinct reluctance by the government to confer it. For decades, on the identity cards of Kurdish citizens, "under review" has been written in the space for "citizenship." Stateless and insecure, Kurds gravitate to the tough world of undocumented manual labor. In *Little Mountain*, the fictional portrait of Beirut by the country's preeminent novelist, Elias Khoury, Kurds always appear as faceless toilers and random victims: "In every street, there was a machine, Syrian and Kurdish workers swarming around it, throwing sand, gravel, and water into its entrails"; "Kurdish sorrow was pouring out into the street. We heard only screams that sounded like cries for help."

To drive into the Bekaa Valley, as I did with the young militants of the PKK, is to step into a fertile and intriguing region that is effectively part of "Greater Syria," best known to the world as a place of arms for the "Party of God," Maronite turncoats, Palestinian rejectionists, and others. Less well known to the world is Syria's longstanding dispute with Turkey. In the 1920s and 1930s, Kemal Atatürk succeeded in detaching and annexing the Syrian province of Hatay and the Syrian port of Alexandretta. Today, this older enmity is reinforced by the Turkish construction of the Atatürk Dam, a vast hydroelectric complex. It has the potential to reduce the flow of the Euphrates River across the Syrian border. In return, as Syria is wont to remind Turkey, Damascus can turn "on" or "off" the Kurdish insurgency against Ankara.

Since August 15, 1984, when it declared war on the Turkish state, the PKK has had to fight Iraqi Kurdish volunteers as well as Turkish regular soldiers. Neither the Barzani nor the Talabani forces in Iraq wanted a second front across their trade and military lifeline to Turkey, which would make them prisoners of both Iraq's embargo and the international embargo against Iraq. The situation—Kurds fighting Kurds—encapsulates the horrors and contradictions of Kurdish history.

The commander of this war is one of the last Communist rebels still operating. He has given few interviews and is seldom photographed. Often based in Damascus, he also directs his forces from a fortified camp very deep in the Bekaa. Its entrance is concealed among rocks off a back road; as we arrived there an Israeli jet was streaking overhead, keeping an eye on nearby Palestinian positions. An arch across the dirt road proclaimed the Mahsum Korkmaz Military Academy, named for a PKK Central Committee member who died in a Turkish prison. Inside, smartly uniformed figures marched through a neat, graveled drill square. They looked far more military than any of the scruffy Syrian and Lebanese outfits I had seen along the way (one of which had slyly solicited us for a donation to supplement their meager wages).

One thing struck me right away. Of the several hundred young fighters in the camp, perhaps one-quarter were female. This is almost unheard of among the Pesh Merga of Iraq, whose ranks rarely include women, save maybe a nurse or two. But if the PKK were progressive in this respect, they were decidedly reactionary in another: the very first event I witnessed was a "self-criticism" session, modeled after the Chinese Cultural Revolution, with recruits sitting under a large tent, reciting their own and others' shortcomings. In the adjacent makeshift library, which was overlooked by a well-kept memorial to the martyrs of the party, dusty volumes by Stalin and Zhdanov adorned the shelves.

After a lot of cautioning about "security," I was admitted to see Oçalan. I couldn't shake the impression that I was squeezing the hand of Joseph Stalin himself. With his big teeth, black moustache, and hair *en brosse*, Oçalan perhaps tries to cultivate this very impression. Leaning on his stick and gesturing to a hospitable table of grapes and cheese, he gave a very bright smile that certainly reinforced his avuncular image. Of course, Stalin was also known as "Uncle Joe."

The Kurdish leadership in Iraq, Oçalan told me, was tribal and feudal and based on clan loyalty. In the past these feudalists sold Kurdistan to foreign intervention, and were also used as mercenaries against other oppressed peoples, such as the Armenians. Turkey was trying, with "a combination of panic and intelligence," to fill the power vacuum left by the Desert Storm victory, and to prevent an independent Kurdistan from emerging. Those like Talabani, who called for mere autonomy, were idealists. Independence was the only solution, since "autonomy" would never be conceded in any case. The Kurdish people, he said, are "weak when it comes to ideas, habitually quarrelsome, and have a low cultural level." I had heard such self-criticism from a variety of Kurds before, but seldom with such rancor.

However, things became less clear when I challenged "Apo" for his own position: did he expect to carve out a new state across four borders by Maoist guerrilla warfare? Had he been at the self-criticism session, what would he have said? At this point, he began to sound rather more like a cult leader than a revolutionary. "The struggle for Kurdistan," he told me, "is a struggle that goes on inside my head." Pleased to talk about himself but keeping his answers vague and guarded, he continued: "First I struggled with my family, and then I struggled with religion. The enemy can't understand me or why I have evolved. If I could be understood fully, everyone would attach themselves to me. I win over those who cannot understand by means of the dialectic. For a thousand years the Turkish state has destroyed its rivals. It removed the Greeks and the Armenians. Now—it is afraid of *me*."

This was true in one way. Villagers in Cizre and other parts of Turkish Kurdistan have held "Long Live Apo" rallies to praise a man they have never seen: Apo himself is from a district near Urfa, which he describes as "not particularly Kurdish," and doesn't even claim to speak the language very well. But the authorities in Turkey do fear and detest the PKK and have sent an army and an air force to combat it. The Kurdish leadership in Iraq and the gradually emerging semilegal Kurdish spokesmen in Turkey are eager to distance themselves from Apo and his "extremism." Yet, faced by the eclipse of Leninism, Oçalan sits confidently in his base and trains young fighters who are eager for combat precisely because the situation is so "extreme."

The effect of the PKK's war can be felt far beyond the southeastern provinces. In Ankara, at the fashionable revolving restaurant atop a tower which looms over the city's most Westernized shopping mall, I had lunch with a Turkish employee of a leading Western news service. Like many city dwellers, he had tried to put his "backward" Kurdish ancestry behind him and become an assimilated Turk. But now he was quietly studying the language of his grandparents and had surreptitiously bought an old Kurdish grammar book in the northern Kormanji dialect. He kept in touch with developments in the provinces. "The popular name for the PKK is now simply Karkër—'the workers,'" he told me. "Even those who work on building the Atatürk Dam are secret supporters of Apo, and the party has been smart enough to drop its opposition to the dam, which will benefit the peasants." Indeed, Oçalan told me that the dam will one day be the capital resource of a new Kurdistan, and will therefore no longer menace Syria.

From Beirut I flew to Cyprus, to meet an author whose following is as devoted as it is limited. Mention the name Salim Barakat among literate Kurds and you will be favored with a look of respect. Barakat was born in Qamishli, a predominantly Kurdish town on the Syrian side of the border with Turkey. His father was a mullah, or village holy man, and his mother spoke only Kurdish. The young Salim was expelled from school for claiming to be a Kurd and for speaking in the language of his home—a language that, even now, he can only speak, but not read or write.

Barakat is very much a bohemian. He has converted the idea of statelessness almost into a style. Leaving the harsh conditions of northern Syria, and the arduous rural life depicted in his novel *Sages of Darkness*, he moved to the more cosmopolitan surroundings of Beirut, where he managed to exchange his false papers for Yemeni ones. Drawn to the Palestinian movement by its culture of exile and resistance, he went to work for *Al-Karmel*, the literary magazine edited by the renowned Palestinian poet Mahmoud Darwish. When the Palestinians were driven from Beirut in 1982, Barakat went with them. He secured asylum in Cyprus and coedits the magazine from Nicosia, with Darwish, who works out of Paris.

"There were five brothers and four sisters in my family," he told me. (*Sages of Darkness* is eloquent on the splendors and miseries of a large household.) "Two of my brothers, one older and one younger, are in prison in Syria and we have no news of them. My sisters are in Egypt, Sweden, and Lebanon. My father is dead. My mother is in Damascus with my other brothers." It was tempting to see in this a metaphor for the wrenching and scattering of the Kurds in general. But Barakat didn't emanate self-pity, preferring to talk about the authors who tenant his imagination—Melville, Kafka, and especially Borges. We talked about the Arab writers he doesn't admire so much—Abdelrahman Munif, Naguib Mahfouz—and about Salman Rushdie, whom he does: "In order to be a fantasist, you must be very realistic," he averred.

Kurdistan, however, was never far from his mind. "Did you see that Saddam Hussein didn't even protest when the Turks attacked the Kurds in northern Iraq? Such cynicism." He described what he knew of the fate of the Kurds in Syria, saying that the Assad regime had for the moment abandoned its plans to "relocate" them away from their Turkish and Iraqi kinsmen in the border areas.

Living the life of the *déraciné* author, Barakat strives to avoid Kurdish parochialism but admits that, especially since he recently became a father, he would prefer not to have to move again, or find another residence permit and another passport. The longing for a homeland is with him. He was deeply affected by the mass gassing and poisoning of the Kurds in Iraq and, after the awful news of Halabja, wrote a long poem entitled *Mahabad*, after the doomed republic. To understand the significance of Mahabad, and the whole of Kurdish history, is to see the world from the perspective of the perpetually losing side.

I was reviewing the Kurdish *intifada*—the word used in some regions of Turkey is *seribildan*—with Jalal Talabani in his mountain headquarters in Shaqlawa one afternoon. Down the pitted road was the office of the Communist Party, and on every wall in the town there were posters and political proclamations. A vivid, open debate was going on in a region that had long been regimented, bullied, and stifled. One of the best-known public disagreements was between Talabani and Massoud Barzani, about the extent to which negotiations with Saddam Hussein were decent or permissible. This in turn raised the issue of Kirkuk, the center of the oilfields and the possible key to a future Kurdish economy. "We can never give up Kirkuk," said Talabani. "It is our Jerusalem."

His analogy was a suggestive one. It is not as if Kirkuk is sacred to any religion. But in the towns of northern Iraq, like Zakho, Dahuk, and Halabja, there are still people who refer to certain streets and homes as "the Jewish quarter." And, as is often forgotten, Baghdad itself was within living memory a tremendous source and center of Jewish culture. (My collaborator, Ed Kashi, is the son of two Baghdad-born Jews who lived there at a time when the city was almost one-third Jewish.)

The Iraqi Jewish diaspora did not end happily. It was reduced to a small, insecure minority by the competing pressures of Arab chauvinism and proselytizing Zionism (some of whose agents were not above encouraging emigration by bombing synagogues). Iraqi Jews in Israel generally do not have warm memories of their old home. But in the search for the missing Jews of Kurdistan I found that those who quit this odd and difficult terrain a generation or two ago are still nostalgic for it. There was an echo of the long rhythms of the Babylonian exile in the following statement from the National Organization of the Jews of Kurdistan, issued in Jerusalem on the annual Sehrane holiday, which is celebrated with music and folk dancing during the Sukkot festival in October:

In the beginning of the nineteenth century, the first Jews from Kurdistan immigrated to the Land of Israel and settled in the ancient city of Jerusalem (1812). In the current century a large immigration of Jews from Kurdistan began in the twenties and thirties. The main group of Kurdish Jews immigrated to Israel after the establishment of the state. . . . It is important to emphasize that this massive immigration was caused by Zionist motivation and not because of anti-Semitism or religious or national persecution.

The Kurds of Jerusalem were generally true to this precept; holding special events in the aftermath of the Gulf War to raise money for the relief of their stricken former kinsmen in northern Iraq. Kurdi, as they are known locally, are found at all levels of Israeli society. In the Jerusalem municipality, for example, they range from former mayor Teddy Kollek's driver to Aharon Sarig, who is one of those responsible for administering Arab affairs in the city. His family came on donkeys from Kurdistan to Palestine in 1935, after his father had been forcibly conscripted into the Ottoman Turkish army, taken prisoner by the British, and interned in India. Sarig told me that there are approximately 100,000 Kurdish Jews in Israel—some from Iran but most, like him, from northern Iraq. At a splendid Kurdish lunch I met several more leading Kurdish Jews, such as Haviv Shimoni, the dues collector for the Jerusalem office of the Histradut, Israel's powerful labor-union federation, and publisher of *Hithatchut* (Renewal), a magazine of Kurdish life.

In the post–Desert Storm interregnum, it would actually be possible for a Kurdish Israeli Jew to travel to Turkey, cross the Iraqi border, and visit Dahuk or Zakho again, a contingency that for decades had been as remote as a voyage to Mars. At this table in Jerusalem, it was fascinating to hear these middle-aged men talk about the possibility of a return, however brief, to the scenes of their boyhood.

The last country of the Kurdish diaspora that I was able to visit was Syria. The capital, Damascus, which is purportedly the oldest continuously inhabited city in the world, is also a melting-pot of minorities. Within its compass can be found neighborhoods and communities of Circassians, Druzes, Yazidis, Kurds, Jews, Alawites, and Armenians. The Kurds number approximately one million. The government of President Hafez al-Assad is largely composed of adherents of the minority Alawi sect. Various twists in the game of nations—Assad's enmity toward Saddam Hussein; his rivalry with Turkey; his uneasy alliance with Iran—have created opportunities and openings for Kurdish life in Syria.

It was in Damascus that the imperishable Saladin chose to be buried. His tomb is just outside the magnificent Omayyad Mosque and bears an inscription recording its refurbishment in 1898 during the visit of Kaiser Wilhelm II, who was an influential player in the region in his time. The ten thousand Kurdish warriors who had come with Saladin to defend Islam are all said to have asked to "stay on" after his death and be buried in Damascus also. They were settled on a hillside overlooking the city, which is known to the present day as the Hay al-Akrad, or Kurdish quarter. Most of the Kurdish allusions and usages in this area date from the Crusader period. The most famous of the Crusader castles—the great chain of fortresses that extends through the Levant—is called by Western chroniclers Krak des Chevaliers. But its local Arabic name is Husn al-Akrad, or "Castle of the Kurds."

While strolling in the Kurdish quarter one afternoon, I came upon the Saladin mosque. A number of Kurds were among the afternoon worshippers. They told me stories that I would hear repeated throughout the country: that here they were freer by far than they would be in Iraq or Turkey; that Syria had accepted some refugees from Iraq's genocidal campaign, as it had from Turkey in the 1920s; that in the "elections" of 1991 no less than fifteen Kurds had been elected to Syria's rubber-stamp parliament. On the other hand, few were willing to give their names, and some had memories of the period of persecution and "Arabization" which ended officially in 1976 only when the government plan to "relocate" border populations had been abandoned. The parliament, like the ruling Ba'ath Party, was a one-man monopoly. Even now, the regime was nervous and had police informers everywhere.

I found similar ambivalence among the spokesmen of Iraqi Kurdish groups living as exiles under temporary Syrian protection. An "election" for President Assad was in progress, and he appeared headed for his fourth straight victory with 99 percent of the vote. "None of these Arab states is a democracy," one of the spokesmen remarked sourly.

Nonetheless, outside the capital it was possible to find Kurdish communities peacefully tending their land as they had done for generations. A few miles north of Aleppo, a Sunni Arab guide led me to the top of a hill which bore one of the most marvelous early Christian sites in the world: the church where Saint Simeon Stylites had drawn pilgrims to his solitary pillar. The imposing ruin, which mingled the Byzantine with the Latin, stood among a fine copse of trees and overlooked a broad expanse of fields and villages. Gesturing down

with a sweep of his arm, the guide exclaimed, "Kurds!" We were looking at the Kurd Dagh, ancestral territory of Saladin's warriors. Kurdish is still spoken here, but it is heavily inflected with Arabic, and the typical villager is as likely to identify himself as Syrian as anything else.

In Aleppo itself there is slightly more nationalism in the air. Many of the inhabitants are Armenian refugees from Turkey who sympathize with the Kurdish struggle on principle. I asked Armen Mazloumian, proprietor of the city's famous Baron's Hotel (Agatha Christie wrote *Murder on the Orient Express* in one of the rooms, and T. E. Lawrence stayed there), if he could introduce me to any local Kurds. That was when I met Jamal the waiter, a strong supporter of the PKK and an ardent nationalist.

The Syrian regime itself, as I discovered, is as ambivalent as the Kurds are. Bureaucrats in the Information Ministry wondered openly what I was doing as they fingered the stamp of my exit permit. "We have no problem with the Kurds. So why are you interested in them? Why not write about the Kurds in Turkey or Iraq?" Did I have any requests for interviews? Yes, I wanted to meet Khaled Baqdash, the veteran leader of the Syrian Communist Party, who had been one of the great hell-raisers of the Arab world in the fifties and sixties and who was, like most party leaders, a Kurd. "We shall see."

On my return from the north I received a call. "We cannot arrange for you to meet Khaled Baqdash. But you may see his wife, who is also a Communist."

"Is she Kurdish?" I asked.

"No."

This seemed unpromising. It reminded me of Kurdish complaints about Syria's insensitivity to their identity—indifferent to the teaching of the language and occasionally forgetful, like Lebanon, of the need for ID cards and passports.

Still, Syria's record compares very well with Iran's. Ever since the demise of the Mahabad Republic, Iranian Kurds have had to fight for the most perfunctory recognition of their rights. The regime of the Shah considered them subversive (except when they were making themselves a nuisance to Saddam Hussein) and regarded them as obstacles in the path of the Pahlavi version of "modernization." After the Iranian revolution of 1979, in which the Kurds participated and from which they took encouragement, there came the war with Iraq and the hijacking of the state by a cleric-dominated elite. The Khomeini dictatorship proved to be in many ways more ruthless than the Shah's had been, and a vicious war against the Kurds has been in progress ever since it took power.

A trademark of the rule of the mullahs has been the threat of or use of assassination. Iranian exiles and dissidents have been murdered in Paris, while two translators and a publisher of Salman Rushdie's *The Satanic Verses* have been attacked in Italy, Japan, and Norway. Nor have the Kurds been spared this tactic. Dr. Abdolrahman Qassemlou, a veteran nationalist intellectual and the leader of the Iranian Kurdish Democratic Party (IKDP), was murdered in Vienna in July 1989, having been lured to the city by a promise of peace negotiations with the Tehran government. Two of his close associates were also slain. In 1993 in Berlin, a similar fate (with even clearer footprints leading back to Tehran) befell three IKDP leaders who were in the city for a meeting with the Socialist International. As an ethnic minority, the Iranian Kurds, like their Iraqi cousins, can too easily be accused of siding with enemy countries in time of war, and persecuted as such. Thus, for many Kurds, the only solution to their plight is a sovereign Kurdistan.

A Kurdish nation would be a sizable one, incorporating perhaps 22 percent of the population of Iraq, 20 percent of the population of Turkey, 10 percent of the population of Iran, and 7 percent of the population of Syria. It would also include significant minorities in Lebanon and the former Caucasian republics of the USSR, and large settlements of refugee and migrant workers in Europe, were they to emigrate to a new homeland. But the task is fraught with complexities. The Kurds are very fractured politically. They have become diluted ethnically and culturally. They lack a unified grammar and common vernacular. Their subject status has perpetuated divisions, which in turn have been used to perpetuate their subject status.

The Kurds preserve among themselves the religious pluralism that existed before monotheism conquered their region. The majority of Kurds, especially in Iraq, are Sunni and conform to the tenets of the majority of Arab Islam. But in Turkey they often profess one or another form of Shi'ism, including the Alawi and Alevi versions. Iranian Kurds are almost without exception Shi'ite. Thus, like many minorities in history, they tend to correspond to the prevailing status quo faith.

While I was in Diyarbakir, my Kurdish friend Ibrahim Çalan was able to take me on a religious guided tour of the city. There, both Kurds and Armenians claim land and title that was lost to them when the Ottomans collapsed. Elderly men admitted me into semi-abandoned places of worship to show me the Kurdish influence upon all of the old religions, and vice versa. I saw the Church of Mother Mary, founded around A.D. 250, where Christians still conduct their liturgy in Aramaic—the language of Jesus. Aramaic is flecked with Kurdish words, according to Father Aykurt, who has no great love for Kurdish or any other kind of nationalism. The Great Mosque in Diyarbakir shows Zoroastrian influence in its design, including some of the swastika-like Aryan symbols. A Kurdish-speaking Armenian caretaker opened up the Chaldean church for us. (The Armenian church itself was a noble ruin.) Most fascinating of all, I met a Yazidi whose faith combined elements of Judaism, Islam, and Sufism. The old man was chiefly concerned to make two points: one, that the Yazidis are *not* devil worshippers ("we worship the god in all men and all true religion"), as their enemies have always claimed; two, that he regarded himself as a Kurd and not a Turk.

As for language and its confusions, the Kurds of the Turkish-Iraqi border region and the former Soviet Union speak Kormanji, while those to the south of that border speak Sorani. (This does not include three or four subdialects in remote parts of Iran and Turkey.) During my trip, the further south I drove, the less easily my Turkish-Kurdish companions could communicate with others. Kurds of all classes were very sensitive on this point, as if the lack of a strong linguistic bond made them seem provincial.

Even for literate Kurds, this lack is evident in the dearth of standard Kurdish lexicons throughout the world. Oxford University Press published the *Kurdish-English Dictionary*, the result of a joint effort by English philologists and the Iraqi Ministry of Education, in 1966. At the Institut Kurde in Paris, scholars are now laboring on the standardization of the Kurdish alphabet and its transcription from Latin, Arabic, and Cyrillic characters. A small hint of the problem that confronts them: there is only one Kurdish-French dictionary now extant, and that was published in St. Petersburg in 1869. It contained only 15,000 words. The Institut Kurde has expanded the lexicon to 50,000 words.

The problem the Kurds face was put to me very aptly by a group of Iraqi Kurdish writers, who were trying to foster a common culture and a common language for use in a future Kurdistan. Their leader was Dr. Jamal R. Ahmed, who until the Kurdish revolt of 1991 had been lecturerer in Oriental history at Saladin University in the city of Arbil (now one of the disputed border towns between the Pesh Merga and the Iraqi army). "The word 'Arab,'" he told me, "used to mean 'nomad.' Now it is the name of a nation which consists of several states. Our definition of our Kurdishness has the same kinds of possibility—the process begins when we insist we are Kurds. And we do not want more than one state. Many of us would settle for autonomy if we could keep our culture unmolested."

At the time of this writing, the nearest approximation to such a solution is the autonomous Kurdish region of northern Iraq, which leads a nervous existence as the ward of the remaining Western forces based in southeastern Turkey. This embryonic Kurdistan has already lasted longer than the Republic of Mahabad, but it is confronted with a daunting series of difficulties. If a new nation were to be born of a foreign-dictated partitioning of Iraq, it would appear to be a puppet of Western interests. Conversely, however, the Kurds cannot trust Saddam Hussein not to renew his assault on them in the event of an Allied withdrawal. (Significantly, the governments of Syria, Iran, and Turkey forgot their own considerable differences in early 1993, and issued a joint communiqué warning against any break-up of the territorial integrity of Iraq.)

There is, however, a more hopeful sense in which the mini-Kurdistan might set a regional precedent. In 1992, free elections were held in the Kurdish zone, and were certified by international observers. This was the first free election ever to be held on Iraqi soil. Political debate is relatively unfettered in Kurdistan, and democratic forces from the rest of Iraq have taken to holding their meetings and discussions there. The battle for Kurdish freedoms has now become inextricable from the growth and develpment of pluralistic ideas in Iraq,

and perhaps beyond. I remember my Syrian Kurdish friend who lamented the farce of an election in Damascus. I recall the role played by the Kurdish resistance in loosening the rule of the military dictatorship in Turkey, while the connection between Kurdish rights and human rights in Iran could hardly be clearer.

An important condition of the election of an assembly in Iraqi Kurdistan was the allocation of reserved seats for non-Kurdish minorities—mainly Assyrian and other Christians. The attempts at nation-building in the Middle East have usually bungled two great issues: minority rights and the rights of non-Muslims. It is at least possible that the Kurdish example of democracy and secularism may prove infectious. Clearly there are existing regimes who fear the possibility.

The Kurdish list of distinctions is a melancholy one so far: the largest population without a state; time and again, a salient example of the operations of divide-and-rule; one of the most vivid instances of post-Nuremburg genocide; a most celebrated record of warlordism, tribalism, and factionalism. The example of Free Kurdistan is at least a partial transcendence of these. As a people who have been repeatedly taken up and dropped by the international community, the Kurds surely have a claim on the world's sympathy and solidarity as they attempt to build a new nation.

Washington, D.C., 1993

✳ CHRONOLOGY

by Maya Brisley

The Kurds have been living in the region known today as Kurdistan for thousands of years, and many scholars consider the Kurds to be Aryan descendants of the Medes of prebiblical times. The ancient Medes were an Iranian people who, in the twentieth century B.C., moved down from Central Asia and settled in the Zagros Mountains and around Lake Orumiyeh in what is now the Iranian province of West Azerbaijan. The Medes conquered the Assyrian Empire and the great cities of Nimrud and Nineveh, near present-day Mosul, Iraq, but they were in turn defeated by the Persians. Xenophon (400 B.C.) mentions in the *Anabasis* the word "Karduchoi" or "Kardykai," referring to a mountain people who harassed the retreating troops in their march toward the sea. Another strand of Kurdish history traces back to the Scythians, an Indo-European people who moved from what is now the Ukraine and established a kingdom in Iranian Kurdistan.

Historically, the Kurdish calendar dates from the defeat of the Assyrian Empire at Nineveh, north of Mosul, by the forces of the Medes. The Kurdish New Year, or "Newroz," is still celebrated on March 21 and serves to mark the anniversary of the overthrow of the tyrant Zahhak, a thousand years before the coming of Islam.

In 1181 Saladin the Kurd became the sultan of a new dynasty, the Ayyubids, which posed a powerful threat to the Crusader kingdoms of the East. This dynasty extended to the plains of Persia and reached almost to Rey, near present-day Tehran. During his reign, Saladin conquered Jerusalem and most of the Holy Land. The dynasty he founded lasted over seven decades, eventually falling in 1250 when the Mamluk slaves who had been brought from Asia to defend the dynasty took power in Egypt. In the early Middle Ages, the Kurds rivaled the Turks, Persians, and Arabs in their cultural and military prowess in the Muslim world. The development and expansion of the Kurdish empire might have been greater had it not been for the Mongol invasion of the Middle East.

Through the centuries, even up to the present day, Kurds have repeatedly been victimized because of their precarious geographic location. Sandwiched between the great warring civilizations of the Turks, Arabs, and Persians, and in the path of invaders from farther afield, Kurdistan has stood at the crossroads of history and has fought for its independence throughout time.

7th century First record of Kurdish writing.

7th–9th centuries Kurds convert to Islam.

10th–12th centuries Emergence of independent Kurdish principalities: to the north the Chaddadides (951–1174), to the south the Hassanwaihides (959–1015), to the west the Merwanides (990–1096) with their capital in Diyarbakir.

1169–1250 The Kurdish Ayyubid dynasty, founded by Saladin.

14th–15th centuries Reconstitution of the Kurdish principalities following the tidal wave of the Mongol invasion.

1695 Ehmede Khani (born 1651), poet, philosopher, and linguist, publishes his epic, *Mem-o-Zin*, a saga of the Kurdish people calling for the creation of a united nation of Kurdistan.

19th century The Kurdish feudalists rise up against the Ottomans in a series of disconnected revolts (1806). Apart from a few provinces annexed to Persia, all Kurdish territories come under firm Ottoman rule.

1898 The first Kurdish journal, *Kurdistan*, appears and begins to propagate the idea of a Kurdistan national liberation movement.

1908 The Young Turk Revolt. The Young Turks begin to apply repressive policies against non-Turkish peoples, including the Albanians, Armenians, and Kurds.

April 19–26, 1920 The San Remo Conference. In the aftermath of World War I, Britain is given a mandate over Arab Iraq and the Kurdish vilayet (administrative region) of Mosul, "ceded" by France in exchange for Cilicia. There is talk of creating separate Armenian and Kurdish states in the territories which had originally been allocated to Russia.

1919–1920 The first Kurdish revolt against the British occupation of southern Kurdistan (Iraq), led by Sheikh Mahmoud.

August 10, 1920 The Treaty of Sèvres confirms the borders defined at San Remo. Section II (Articles 62–64) envisages the creation of a Kurdish state on the Kurdish territory.

October 20, 1921 The French and Turks sign the Ankara Agreement. France takes the Kurdish provinces of Jezireh and Kurd Dagh, which are annexed under the Syrian mandate.

August 27, 1921 Sir Percy Cox, the British high commissioner of Mesopotamia, presents the throne of Iraq to Emir Faisal, son of the sherif of Mecca, whom the French had just expelled from Syria. The Kurds of Mosul boycott the plebiscite organized to "elect" Faisal under the banner "Since when are kings elected?"

1923 Sheikh Mahmoud leads a second revolt, proclaims himself "king of Kurdistan," and establishes contact with Simko, the leader since 1920 of a Kurdish revolt against Persian domination. The movement is repressed by the British Army, and the sheikh is exiled to India.

March 3, 1923 The seal is set on the annexation of most of Kurdistan by the new Turkish Republic, led by its founding father, Mustafa Kemal Atatürk. The headwaters of the Euphrates and Tigris rivers emanate in Kurdistan, so the Kurds also lose any share of their ancestral water riches.

March 3, 1924 A Turkish decree bans all Kurdish schools, organizations, and publications, along with the religious fraternities (*tekke*) and religious schools (*medresse*).

February–April 1925 The council of the League of Nations accepts the British claim to annex southern Kurdistan (Mosul and Kirkuk) under the Iraqi mandate, thereby robbing the Kurds of their ancestral claims to that oil-rich area.

August 1927 Hoyboun (Independence), the Kurdish National League, is founded to bring together all Kurdish political parties and organizations following World War I.

1928 The entire civil and military administration of Kurdistan in Turkey is entrusted to the inspector general of the East, the Turkish high commissioner for Kurdistan. Revolts erupt throughout the Kurdish provinces.

June 1930 Simko, the leader of the Kurdish revolt against the central authority of Iran since 1920, is assassinated during talks with representatives of Tehran.

1931 Revolts break out in Iranian Kurdistan under Jafar Sultan and in Iraqi Kurdistan under Sheikh Mahmoud.

May 1932 Ankara promulgates a law for the deportation and dispersion of the Kurds to non-Kurdish western Turkey, following a fascist trend in Germany and Italy to depopulate areas with restive minorities.

1933 Led by Mullah Mustafa Barzani, the Kurds rise up in Iraq.

1936–1938 Armed resistance by the Kurds in Dersim (Turkish Kurdistan) erupts against the Turks' repressive authority.

1943–1945 Kurdish revolt in Iraq continues under the leadership of Mullah Mustafa Barzani, who is eventually forced to retreat into Iranian Kurdistan.

August 1945 The Iranian Kurdish Democratic Party (IKDP) is founded by a group of communist Kurds.

January 13, 1946 The short-lived Kurdish Republic is proclaimed at Mahabad (Iranian Kurdistan).

March 1947 The leaders of the Mahabad Kurdish Republic are hanged by the Iranian government at a public execution.

1956 Turkey, Iran, and Iraq sign the Baghdad Pact, creating a more coordinated defense against the disparate Kurdish revolts and movements.

July 14, 1958 A military coup led by General Kassem overthrows the Iraqi monarchy.

May 27, 1960 A military coup overthrows the Menderes government in Turkey.

September 11, 1961 Beginning of a Kurdish armed uprising in Iraq, led by Mullah Mustafa Barzani. The Iraqi army launches its first major offensive against the Kurds in mountainous terrain.

June 18, 1963 The USSR officially declares its support for the Kurdish uprising and Barzani's group.

February 10, 1964 Marshal Aref, commander of Iraqi armed forces fighting the Kurdish uprising, recognizes Kurdish national rights.

March 1965 Military operations begin again in Iraq and continue until the second cease-fire in June 1966.

1967–1968 Kurdish peasants wage tactical guerrilla war in Iranian Kurdistan.

July 30, 1968 Saddam Hussein becomes deputy chairman of the Revolutionary Command Council of the Ba'ath Party in Iraq, and his portfolio is expanded to head internal security.

August 8, 1969 The Kurdish village of Dakan in Mosul, Iraq, is the scene of a major army atrocity. The war against the Kurds in Iraq is stepped up.

March 11, 1970 The Kurds and the Iraqi government sign an agreement on the "Autonomy of Kurdistan," to be implemented within four years, and the fighting stops.

March 12, 1970 In what is regarded as the most brutal military coup in modern Turkey, center-left and left-wing democratic parties and organizations are outlawed en masse. Thousands of Kurdish separatists and nationalists, students, trade unionists, and members of the intelligentsia are among those arrested and brought before special military tribunals.

March 1974 Following the collapse of the 1970 Kurdish autonomy accords in Iraq, war breaks out. The Kurdish towns of Zakho and Qala Diza are razed to the ground. Hundreds of thousands of Kurds flee the cities and brutalities break all previous records.

March 6, 1975 The Algiers Agreement between the Iraqi Ba'ath Party headed by Saddam Hussein and the Shah's regime in Iran is promulgated. Iraq formally concedes to Iranian territorial demands in return for the Shah ending support for the Iraqi Kurdish rebels. With their supply lines cut, the Kurdish resistance crumbles and the Iraqi government launches its policy of mass deportations and resettlement.

March 1975 The Iraqi Kurdish leadership flees to Iran.

June 1976 A new phase of guerrilla (Pesh Merga) operations is launched in Iraqi Kurdistan to stop the brutal Iraqi campaign against the Kurds and their towns and villages.

1978 The Kurdistan Workers Party (PKK) is formed by Abdullah Öçalan, a Turkish Kurd.

February 10–11, 1979 The monarchy is overthrown in Iran. In Kurdistan, Kurdish partisans seize army barracks and police stations, and set up a de facto autonomous administration.

March 1979 The Kurdish provinces in Iran boycott the referendum on forming the Islamic Republic. Violent incidents at Naghadeh are followed by a series of clashes, which culminate in August with the Iranian army's massive general offensive against the Kurdish autonomous forces.

June 1979 Saddam Hussein becomes president of Iraq.

August 17, 1979 Ayatollah Khomeini declares war on the Kurds. The Iranian Islamic Army re-occupies every Kurdish town.

September–October 1979 Kurdish guerrilla operations are carried out throughout Iranian Kurdistan.

August 15, 1984 The PKK starts its guerrilla warfare against the Turkish state in southeastern Anatolia.

March 1988 "The Massacre of the Innocents." Iraq uses chemical weapons in the Iraqi Kurdish town of Halabja and over 5,000 Kurds perish in one afternoon. This marks the beginning of the *anfal*, a genocidal campaign against the Kurds of Iraq which eventually took more than 180,000 lives and destroyed over 4,000 Kurdish towns and villages.

March 1991 In the aftermath of the Gulf War and the failed uprising of the Iraqi Kurds against the battered Iraqi regime, Saddam's forces attack Kurds and send over one million fleeing to the mountains of Iran and Turkey.

April 1991 The U.S.-led Allied Operation Provide Comfort begins setting up camps and bringing supplies to hundreds of thousands of Kurds stranded in the mountains. A "safe haven" is established by the United States and Britain above the 36th parallel in Iraq, and the tenuous birth of Iraqi Kurdistan follows.

June 1992 Democratic elections are held in Iraqi Kurdistan. Thousands wait for hours at polling stations to cast their ballots. The Kurds create the only democratic parliament and government in the region, but must continue to endure Iraqi threats and a stifling embargo by Baghdad of fuel and food supplies.

March 1992 The massacre of Kurdish townspeople in Cizre by the Turkish army during Newroz (New Year's) celebrations.

Summer 1992 The PKK steps up its attacks on Turkish targets, bringing the total deaths since 1984 to over five thousand.

October 1992 Turkish armed forces move into Iraqi Kurdistan, and with the approval of the Iraqi Kurdish Pesh Merga, a joint operation against the PKK guerrillas commences. The PKK, encircled, agrees to lay down arms and surrender to the Pesh Merga. Iraqi Kurdish leadership allows unarmed PKK guerrillas to remain in designated mountain camps in the region.

March 1993 Abdullah Oçalan, leader of the PKK, announces a unilateral cease-fire with Turkey. Stating that he wants to seek a political solution, he urges the Turkish government to introduce a federal system that would give Kurds more political influence.

June 1993 The Turkish government in Ankara ignores the PKK's peace overtures and resumes attacks on Kurdish guerrilla camps along the Iranian border.

July 1993 Kurdish militants, under the direction of the PKK, launch attacks and take hostages at Turkish consulates, embassies, and businesses across Europe. They give up after one day, but claim success at having garnered worldwide media attention.

1992–1993   More than sixteen journalists are killed in southeastern Turkey while covering the Kurdish situation.

November 1993   The PKK is banned in Germany and France. All PKK offices raided by police and activities of Kurdistan Solidarity Committee halted.

1993–Present   All Turkish newspapers, magazines, and other publications banned from mentioning or interviewing PKK members.

January 1994   All leaves suspended for Turkish military personnel, including the highest-ranking officers.

WHEN THE BORDERS BLEED

Having fled their war-torn home near Kirkuk, Iraq, a Kurdish family battle the elements in the ruins of Penjwin, on the border with Iran. Hostile neighbors and forbidding weather conspire against the Kurds in their struggle to reclaim their homeland.

Penjwin, one of thousands of Kurdish towns destroyed by Iraqi forces, provides little shelter for this family. A mountain people, the Kurds manage to survive subzero winter temperatures while living in tents with no heat, water, or electricity.

Amidst the stunningly beautiful mountains of Iraqi Kurdistan, the town of Said Sadiq lies in ruins from Iraq's campaign of destruction. Some Kurds now live in reconstructed huts and UN housing, but until there is real security they will not rebuild.

Boys run through the remnants of Qala Diza, an Iraqi Kurdish city near the border with Iran. Following the Iran-Iraq war, Saddam Hussein's troops gave the residents of Qala Diza only a few hours to evacuate the city before they bombed, dynamited, or bulldozed every building. Of the original population of over 100,000, only some 20,000 returned after the Gulf War.

Lives hang in the balance in what is left of Qala Diza. The Iraqi government has imposed a strict blockade of food and fuel to the region known as Free Kurdistan, where families struggle to rebuild amid the wreckage.

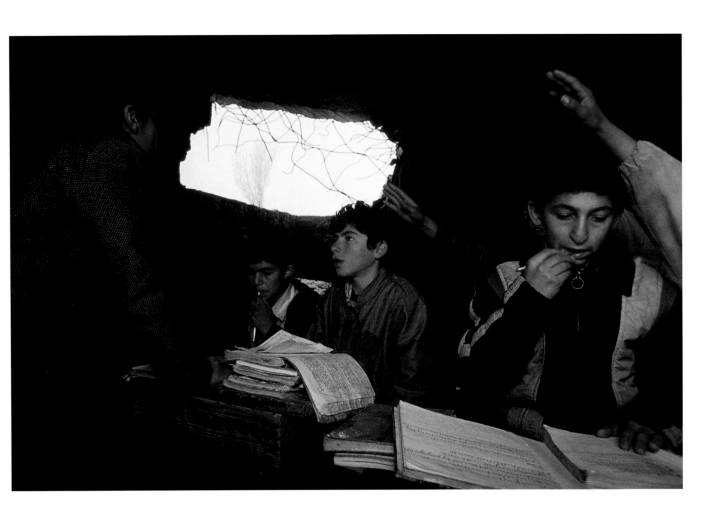

Even harsh winter conditions don't stop these brave children from attending school. In bombed-out schoolrooms in Penjwin, Kurdish children study in three daily shifts because there aren't enough teachers, rooms, or supplies.

Throughout Iraqi Kurdistan, students are finally studying Kurdish history, which was forbidden under Iraqi rule. It is the only place in Kurdistan where classes are held in Kurdish. Without the money to print their own textbooks, students are forced to make do with what the Iraqis left behind, sometimes filling up notebooks and erasing them to be used again.

Baking traditional Kurdish bread in the ruins of what was once a house in Qala Diza, Iraq.

In Halabja, Iraq, a Kurdish guerrilla inspects an unexploded chemical bomb from the 1988 attack that killed some five thousand Kurds. Although Saddam Hussein denied the use of chemical warfare against the Kurds, this event was the turning point in raising international awareness of the genocidal campaign that was taking place.

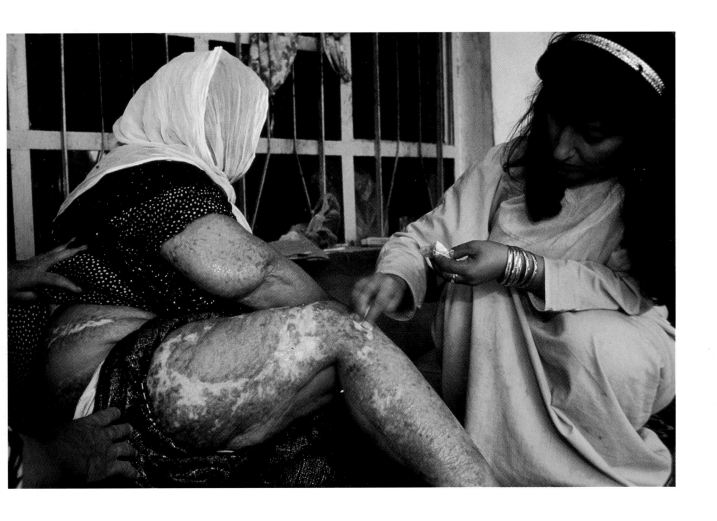

This fifty-four-year-old woman wears the scars of Halabja, an Iraqi town that was annihilated by poison gas in 1988. Twenty-five of her relatives died in the attack, and now her daughter attends to wounds that continue to burn three years later.

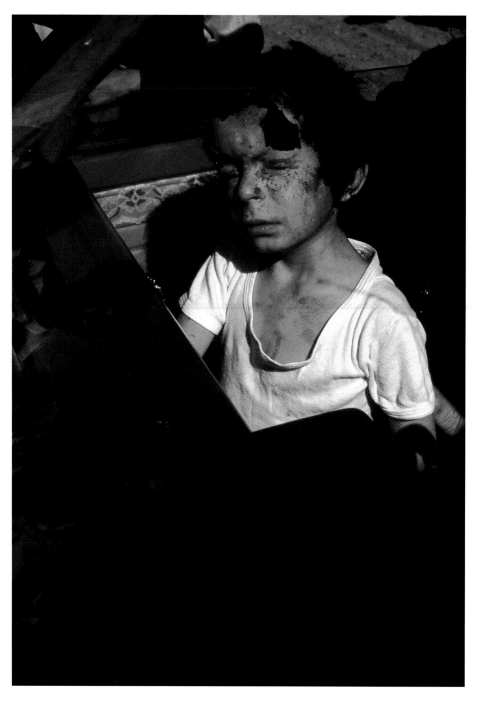

This seven-year-old boy was blinded by an Iraqi phosphorus bomb. The Iraqi army dropped bombs on fleeing Kurds after the failed Kurdish uprising in the wake of the Gulf War.

In the city of Dahuk, Iraq, young men join a demonstration to encourage the United Nations to continue its support in northern Iraq. "Where is my brother?" ask the words on one man's chest, referring to the 200,000 Kurds who are dead or missing since the mid-1970s.

A mother washes her baby near the remains of their bulldozed home in Qala Diza.

A tourist rest stop in northern Iraq serves as a shelter for Kurdish refugees, who have returned from camps in Turkey but are afraid to go deeper into Iraq to their hometowns.

A Kurdish meat seller finds his way home in the darkness of Penjwin.

Dynamited and bulldozed by Iraqi forces in 1989, the modern city of Qala Diza has no running water, electricity, or sewerage, so these Kurdish women have to draw water from a nearby stream. Qala Diza is just one of four thousand towns and villages destroyed by Saddam's forces since the mid-1970s.

A refugee washes his feet at the Yemishli camp on the border of Iraq and Turkey.

Father and son take a stroll through the Yemishli camp, which held 60,000 refugees at the height of the crisis in the spring of 1991.

More than 60,000 Kurdish refugees live in Iran's Khoy camp in the province of Azerbaijan. Iran assists the Iraqi Kurds in part to pacify its own restive Kurdish population, which numbers nearly four million.

Iran has housed Iraqi Kurdish refugees for more than twenty years, and an entire generation has been born and raised under these conditions. In Iran's Ziveh refugee camp, the only home these three sisters have ever known is a plastic tarp.

An Iraqi Kurdish woman (left) grieves for her ten-year-old daughter, who has just been shot and killed by the Turkish army for straying outside the boundaries of the Ishikveren refugee camp. Most of the camp's 200,000 inhabitants walked for days without shoes through snow and ice to find safety after the Gulf War. The Turkish government provided protection for fleeing Iraqi Kurds, but strictly limited their movements.

Dusk settles on the Yemishli camp, where 60,000 refugees fled to escape the Iraqi army's persecution following the Gulf War.

Displaced by Iraqi aggression after the Gulf War, an old Kurdish couple must move once again to another refugee camp in Iraqi Kurdistan.

An Iraqi refugee brings a precious loaf of bread home to his tent in the Ishikveren camp. Ethnic ties outweighed the arbitrary distinction of national borders as Turkish Kurds turned out thousands of loaves of bread each day to help their Iraqi Kurdish neighbors.

Hopeful that their home has not been destroyed by the Iraqi army, a Kurdish family, in transit from Iranian refugee camps on their way home, wait in the Iraqi Kurdish town of Ranyiah.

Refugees from the Ishikveren camp in Turkey are loaded onto a truck for the trip back across the mountains to Iraq. Turkish soldiers make sure that no one strays from the camp or is left behind.

In hospital tents provided by the Turkish Red Crescent, like this one at the Ishikveren refugee camp, the most common symptoms are malnutrition, diarrhea, and exhaustion.

A German helicopter flies in relief supplies to the Ishikveren camp as part of the U.S.-led Allied effort, Operation Provide Comfort, following the Gulf War.

After three fruitless visits to the hospital tent, this family gather around their six-month-old baby, waiting for him to die. He is one of hundreds of babies who died of malnutrition in the Ishikveren camp.

A father buries his six-month-old son while friends and relatives assist in the somber, often-repeated ritual.

The Kurdish village of Baroshki in northern Iraq was destroyed three times over the last two decades by the Iraqi army. Under Allied protection after the Gulf War, the Kurds could finally rebuild their homes, towns, and villages.

Cement sacks are a sign of
growth in Diyarbakir, Turkey,
an important center of
economic activity in a region
where development has been
held back for decades.

Kurdish pensioners gather
outside the partly destroyed
city hall in Zakho, Iraq, to
receive their late payments,
delayed by the disruptions of
war and Saddam's refusal to
honor them.

Lines for fuel and other vital supplies are common in Iraqi Kurdistan because of the Iraqi embargo. Even UN relief trucks carrying fuel, food, and supplies have been attacked on their journey to Kurdistan. These people in Dahuk have been waiting for over a week, in freezing temperatures, for heating oil.

An old man waits for prayers
to begin at the Great Mosque
in Diyarbakir, Turkey.

The Great Mosque in Diyarbakir was converted into a church when the Crusaders conquered the region. Today, although the majority of Kurds are Sunni Muslims, small minorities practice Zoroastrianism, Christianity, and Judaism.

Following the Gulf War, thousands of portraits of Saddam Hussein have been replaced by those of Kurdish heroes. Outside a mural painter's studio in Zakho is the image of Mullah Mustafa Barzani, grandfather of Kurdish nationalism and founder of the Kurdistan Democratic Party, which his son, Massoud, now leads.

Kids and chicks in a Diyarbakir back alley.

Because they have no homeland of their own, the Kurdish leader Massoud Barzani has called his people the "orphans of the universe."

Making tomato paste the old-fashioned way, by letting it bake in the sun on the roof, in the poor district of Ali Pasha, in Diyarbakir.

Near the Turkish border in Iraq, one person's leftovers are another's feast. These women have special permission to scavenge for wheat that the farmer's harvester misses.

Sifting grain on a Diyarbakir
rooftop, with the smoke-
shrouded district of Ali Pasha
in the background.

In the Syrian Kurdish city of Qamashli, near the Turkish border, Kurds and Arabs play dominoes and checkers in a late-night café.

Diyarbakir is the unofficial capital of Turkish Kurdistan; more than 90 percent of its one million residents are Kurdish, which makes it the largest Kurdish city in the world.

A schoolyard in Diyarbakir.

Kurdish boys play soccer in the dusty "wild east" metropolis of Diyarbakir. Looming in the background is a remnant of the black basalt fortress walls that were begun under the Roman emperor Constantine in A.D. 348.

A Turkish policeman keeps watch over Diyarbakir's May Day celebrations, which attract Kurdish militants.

Kurds go to market in Diyarbakir.

Kurdish men in Zakho, Iraq, haggle over the price of sheep in the weekly market.

A tea shop in Diyarbakir.

In a village near Zakho, women mourn the loss of a family elder. Traditionally, the men and women remain isolated from each other during these rituals.

The Kurdish caretaker in a Greek Orthodox church in Istanbul prepares morning tea for her family of ten. Often lacking skills and facing discrimination, the more than three million Kurds in Istanbul must find any means of survival.

Young Kurdish men feel the sting of Turkey's Lake Van, one of the largest saltwater lakes in the world and the origin of much Kurdish folklore.

Flooding from the Atatürk
Dam has claimed thousands of
acres of Kurdish farmland
while creating a stunning
landscape.

This tranquil picnic spot overlooking the Atatürk Dam belies the controversy surrounding this massive project, which will give Turkey absolute control over the Euphrates River and affect the water supplies to Syria and Iraq. Much of this Kurdish family's farmland has been flooded by the dam.

After fleeing from Syria in 1988 to escape political persecution, this family of twelve acclimates its traditional ways to its new home in Cologne, Germany.

The ancient ruins of Hasankeyf, Turkey, are still used as dwellings by the local Kurds. Two boys head home after a dip in the Tigris River, which flows through the town.

Kurdistan spans some 200,000 square miles of mountainous terrain, rich in oil and water. It is currently divided between Turkey, Iraq, Iran, and Syria, and through the millennia it has represented the insurmountable frontier separating the three great civilizations of the region: Persian, Arab, and Turkish.

During its three-thousand-year history, the ancient city of Diyarbakir, Turkey, with its warrens of cobblestone alleyways, has acquired a distinct timelessness.

A mysterious moment in Ali Pasha, the poorest district of Diyarbakir, where Kurdish families live on top of each other in squalid conditions.

A field worker harvests lentils in Syria near the Turkish border. Farms such as this historically belonged to Kurdish landowners until the end of World War I, when the Allies carved up Kurdistan between Turkey, Iraq, Iran, and Syria.

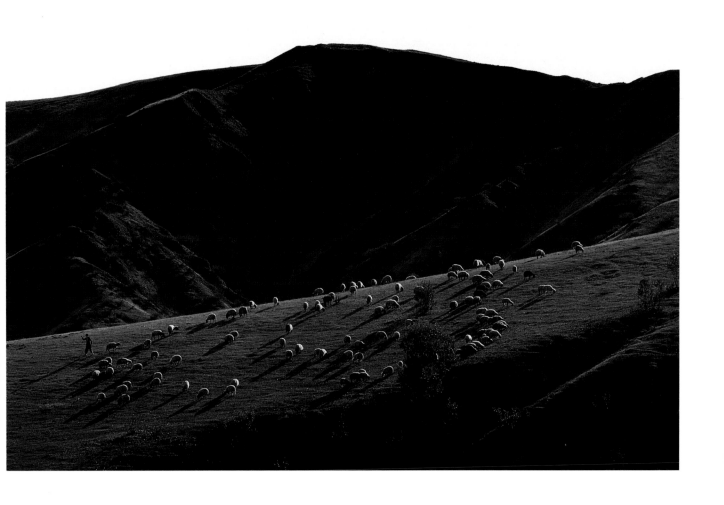

Traditionally nomadic, Kurdish sheepherders have roamed these hills since biblical times.

After months of disruption from the Gulf War, life returns to normal at the weekly sheep market in Zakho, Iraq, from where this man leaves with the latest addition to his flock.

Given the mountainous conditions and harsh winters of Kurdistan, sheepherding has traditionally been a key to Kurdish survival, providing food and clothing. In the Cudi Mountains of Turkey, this sheepherder seems to float on his flock.

Members of the Beritan tribe, the largest nomadic Kurdish family, camp for the summer near Karliova, Turkey. Despite government efforts to force them to settle down, these pastoralists migrate more than five hundred miles round trip between summer and winter pastures.

Nomadic Kurds subsist on milk, yogurt, and other sheep products, which they also sell in the markets of nearby villages.

Blood sacrifice for a prosperous marriage and a bountiful wedding feast greet this Kurdish bridal couple in Turkey as together they pass through the door of the groom's house for the first time.

A light-footed sendoff for a bride in Cizre, Turkey, keeps tradition moving as the celebration proceeds to the groom's house.

A nervous Kurdish bride in the Syrian city of Afrin waits to be chauffeured to the groom's house across town. At Kurdish weddings, even the terms for divorce are prearranged.

At traditional Kurdish
weddings, such as this one in
Van, Turkey, the guests make
offerings to the family of the
groom. When the groom's
father (left) happens to be the
agha, or local chieftain, the
booty can rise above $25,000.
The average per capita income
in southeastern Turkey is less
than $1,000.

107

The *agha*, in feudal times a Kurdish chieftain, is now more like a mafia boss who controls the production of goods and security in his domain. This *agha* in Van works in close association with the Turkish government, and the armed bodyguards that flank him are necessary protection against the PKK, the Kurdistan Workers Party.

Sometimes, the only way a Kurd can be successful is to assimilate. This Kurdish millionaire in Istanbul, who considers himself a Turk first and a Kurd second, became the president of the Turkish Chamber of Commerce, representing more than 700,000 businessmen.

Taking arms against neo-Nazi attacks on foreigners, members of a Kurdish youth gang called the Sioux brandish gas-pellet guns in Berlin's Alexanderplatz. These legal guns are more for effect than fire power.

Gang members horse around in Berlin's subway, a frequent stamping ground. In Berlin alone some five thousand young Kurds have formed gangs for self-defense.

Kurdish New Year festivities, which coincide with the spring equinox, are normally held outdoors to celebrate the end of another forbidding winter. But under the prohibitions on Kurdish culture throughout Kurdistan, the most colorful celebrations are now held in exile. Thousands of Kurds gather in places like this London sports arena to carry on the tradition.

Demonstrators at a PKK rally in Düsseldorf protest Germany's new immigration and asylum laws. With 500,000 Kurds, Germany has the largest Kurdish population outside Kurdistan.

In a Turkish terrorist court in Diyarbakir, this Kurdish woman stands accused of belonging to the violently separatist Kurdistan Workers Party, or PKK, which seeks to create an independent state in southeastern Turkey. Convicted of membership in the outlawed party, she is sentenced to twelve-and-a-half years in prison.

A mother in Diyarbakir holds the portrait of her slain son, who was a member of the PKK. He was killed by the Turkish military in one of their many counterinsurgency campaigns.

On International Children's Day, a Turkish holiday, Kurdish children in a remote village are forced to take part in the festivities while commandos look on from the sidelines.

Living under the pressure of the gun in a remote village of Turkish Kurdistan, a family waits for Turkish commandos to finish a sweep for PKK guerrillas.

At the service of the American 82nd Airborne, these enterprising Kurdish boys make a buck at the temporary base in Silopi, Turkey, during the height of the Allied operation to save the Kurds.

A Kurdish girl and a young American GI are mutually pleased to see each other. Without the Allied presence, Kurdish autonomy and perhaps this young girl's life would be crushed by Saddam Hussein's vengeance.

Iraqi Kurdish guerrillas, called Pesh Merga, take lessons in mortar fire in a captured Iraqi military base.

Pesh Merga practice single-file ground patrols against incursions by the Iraqi army into Free Kurdistan. In the aftermath of the Gulf War, the Kurdish territory north of Iraq's 36th parallel has also been protected by the daily reconnaissance flights of U.S. fighter jets.

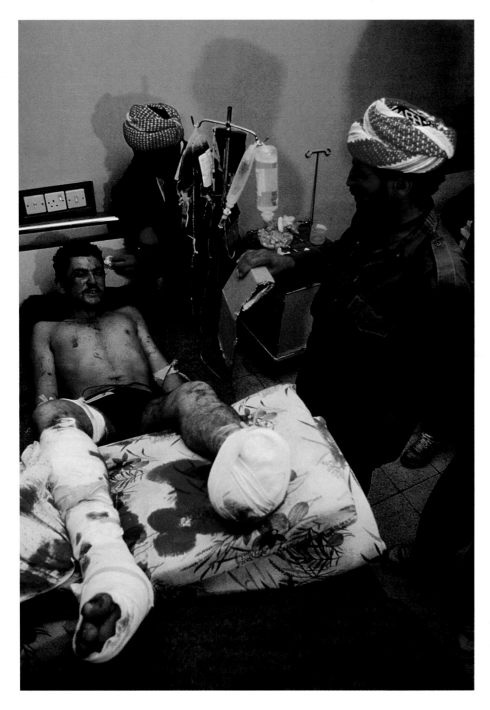

Dying of injuries from an Iraqi mine, a Pesh Merga goes without painkillers while his comrades try to comfort him from the hundred-degree heat in the Zakho hospital.

122

His village destroyed in 1988, this Pesh Merga now lives on a guerrilla base with his countrymen. His face bears the sadness and frustration of decades of loss and oppression, but it also reflects the resolve of the Pesh Merga, whose name means "those who face death."

Even the Pesh Merga have a dress code, and every morning they must go through the meticulous exercise of carefully donning the uniform of baggy pants, cummerbund, and headdress.

Pesh Merga recruits range in age from teenagers to men in their fifties. Their equipment, training, and numbers are no match for the best of the modern Iraqi army. Additional protection is provided by UN relief workers and a small but symbolic security contingent.

Early morning calisthenics for a new group of Pesh Merga recruits in northern Iraq.

Since the UN created a safe haven above the 36th parallel in Iraq, the Kurds have established the largest and most populous area of autonomy in their modern history. Under the direction of two main parties, Massoud Barzani's (left) Kurdistan Democratic Party and Jalal Talabani's Patriotic Union of Kurdistan, democratic elections were held in 1992 to form Kurdistan's first parliament.

In a makeshift court in Zakho, two boys plead their case before a judge (holding the knife). Such courts have sprung up throughout northern Iraq since the Gulf War, administered by the Kurdistan Front coalition, which includes all eight major Kurdish parties in the region. The recently published Federal Declaration of Kurdistan is the first step toward the creation of a truly independent judiciary.

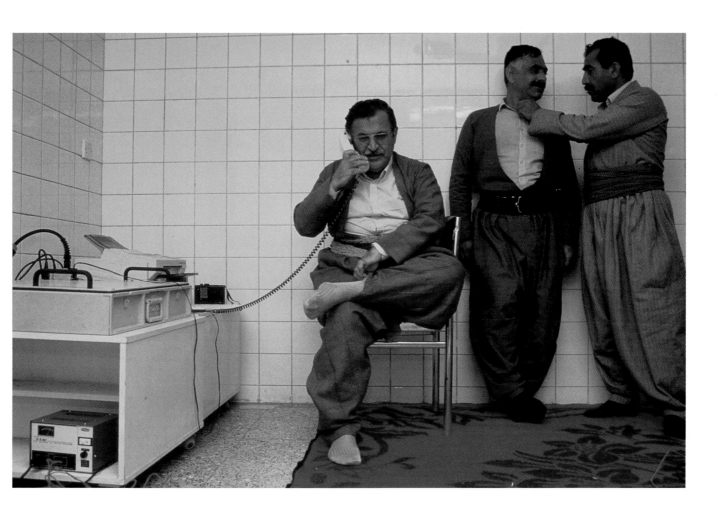

After the Gulf War, Jalal Talabani, leader of the Patriotic Union of Kurdistan, uses the only working telephone in Iraqi Kurdistan.

The PKK are unique among Kurdish guerrilla groups because of their progressive attitude toward education and their inclusion of women as fighters.

In the continual tug of war between Turkey and Iraq over their restive Kurdish populations, this Iraqi Pesh Merga is being pitted against his PKK brothers and sisters. In exchange for allowing relief supplies to enter Iraqi Kurdistan and providing a base for U.S. jets to patrol the region, Turkey expects the Pesh Merga to help control the PKK.

At the end of a three-day rally, zealous supporters line up to shake the hand of Abdullah Oçalan, the Turkish-born founder of the PKK, and kiss his cheek. Some have traveled thousands of miles and risked illegal border crossings for the privilege.

A young supporter of the PKK shouts political slogans during a speech by Oçalan.

Based in a former PLO training camp in Lebanon's Bekaa Valley, the PKK trains arduously for the separatist campaign it is waging in southeastern Turkey. Since 1984, when this campaign began, more than seven thousand people have died in the fighting between the PKK and the Turkish security forces. Syria supports the PKK and uses it as a bargaining chip in water-rights negotiations with Turkey.

For eight hours each day, PKK guerrillas study Kurdish history and socialist ideology.

Twenty thousand gather in
Lebanon's Bekaa Valley for the
annual celebration of the PKK.
Supporters hold up a portrait
of the founder, Abdullah
Oçalan, who is affectionately
called Apo, or "uncle."

137

In and out of Turkish jails for political activities, this ninety-eight-year-old imam lamented that he would not live to see a free Kurdistan; he died in 1992. A political pawn that has been played by Turkey, Iran, Iraq, and Syria, the struggle for Kurdish autonomy is nowhere near resolved.

▒ A SELECT BIBLIOGRAPHY

Alexander, Yonah, and Robert A. Friedlander. *Self-Determination: National, Regional, and Global Dimensions.* Boulder, Colo.: Westview Press, 1980.

Al-Khalil, Samir. *Republic of Fear.* Berkeley and Los Angeles: University of California Press, 1989.

Alter, Peter. *Nationalism.* London and New York: Edward Arnold, 1989.

Arfa, Hassan. *The Kurds: An Historical and Political Study.* London: Oxford University Press, 1966.

Article 19 International Center on Censorship. *Violations of Expression and Information in Turkey: An Article 19 Report.* London, 1990.

————. *Turkey: Censorship by the Bullet: Shocking Statistics and Official Silence.* London, 1992.

Bedir Khan, Sureya. *The Case of Kurdistan Against Turkey.* Philadelphia: Kurdish Independent League, 1928.

Besikci, Ismail. *Selected Writings on Kurdistan and Turkish Colonialism.* London: KSC-KIC Publications, 1991.

————. *The State of Terror in the Middle East.* Ankara: Yurt-Kitap Yayinlari, 1991.

————. *The Tunceli Laws (1935) and the Dersim Genocide.* Bonn: Wesanen Rewsen, 1991.

————. *Kurdistan: An Interstate Colony.* Sydney: Australian Kurdish Association, 1988.

Bois, Thomas. *The Kurds.* Beirut: Khayats, 1965.

Bruinessen, Martin Van. *Agha, Shaikh and State: The Social and Political Structures of Kurdistan.* Utrecht University, 1978; London: Zed Books, 1992.

Bulloch, John, and Harvey Morris. *No Friends but the Mountains: The Tragic History of the Kurds.* London: Viking, 1991.

Chaliand, Gerard. *People Without a Country: The Kurds and Kurdistan.* London: Zed Press, 1980.

————. *Minority Peoples in the Age of Nation States.* London: Pluto Press, 1989.

Cobban, Alfred. *The Nation States and National Self-Determination.* London: Coolins Type Press, 1969.

Crawford, James. *The Rights of Peoples.* Oxford: Clarendon Press, 1988.

Cristescou, Aureliu. *The Right to Self-Determination: Historical and Current Developments on the Basis of United Nations Instruments.* New York: United Nations Publications, 1979.

Dersimi, M. Nuri. *Kurdistan Tarihinde Dersim.* Aleppo: Ani Matbaasi, 1952.

Eagleton, William. *The Kurdish Republic of 1946.* London: Oxford University Press, 1957.

Edip, Halide. *Conflict of East and West in Turkey.* Lahore: Kurdish Institute, University of Lahore, 1935.

Edmonds, C. J. *Kurds, Turks and Arabs: Politics, Travel and Research in North-Eastern Iraq, 1919–1925.* London: Oxford University Press, 1957.

Encyclopedia of Islam. Leiden: E. J. Brill, 1981. Vol. 5, fasc. 85–86, "The Kurds."

Gellner, Ernest. *Nations and Nationalism.* London: Basil Blackwell, 1983.

Ghareeb, Edmund. *The Kurdish Question in Iraq.* Syracuse, N.Y.: Syracuse University Press, 1981.

Ghassemlou, Abdul Rahman. *Kurdistan and the Kurds.* Prague and London: Publishing House of the Czechoslovak Academy of Sciences, 1965.

Gologlu, Mahmut. *Devrimler ve Tepkiler, 1924–1930.* Ankara: Turhan Kitabevi, 1972.

Hannum, Hurst. *Autonomy, Sovereignty and Self-Determination.* Philadelphia: University of Pennsylvania Press, 1990.

Hay, W. R. *Two Years in Kurdistan: Experiences of a Political Officer, 1918–1920.* London: Sedgewick and Jackson, 1921.

Jawad, Sa'ad. *Iraq and the Kurdish Question, 1958–70.* London: Ithaca Press, 1981.

Joarder, Safiuddin. *Syria Under the French Mandate: The*

Early Phase, 1920–1927. Dacca: Asiatic Society of Bangladesh, 1977.

Jwaideh, Wadie. "The Kurdish Nationalist Movement: Its Origins and Development." Ph.D. dissertation, Syracuse University, 1960.

Karpat, Kemal H. *Turkey's Politics: The Transition to a Multiparty System.* Princeton, N.J.: Princeton University Press, 1959.

Keyder, Caglar. *State and Class in Turkey: A Study in Capitalist Development.* London and New York: Verso, 1987.

Kinnane, Derk. *The Kurds and Kurdistan.* London: Oxford University Press, 1964.

Klieman, Aaron S. *Foundations of British Policy in the Arab World: The Cairo Conference of 1921.* Baltimore, Md.: Johns Hopkins University Press, 1970.

Kruger, Karl. *Kemalist Turkey and the Middle East.* London: George Allen and Unwin, 1932.

Laizer, Sheri. *Into Kurdistan: Frontiers Under Fire.* London and Atlantic Highlands, N.J.: Zed Books, 1991.

Louis, William Roger. *The British Empire in the Middle East: 1945–1951.* Oxford: Clarendon Press, 1988.

McCarthy, Justin. *Muslims and Minorities: The Population of Ottoman Anatolia and the End of the Empire.* New York: New York University Press, 1983.

Middle East Watch. *Human Rights in Iraq.* London: Human Rights Watch Books, 1990.

The Minority Rights Group, and David McDowall. *The Kurds: Report No. 23.* London, 1989.

Monroe, Elisabeth. *Britain's Moment in the Middle East.* Baltimore, Md.: Johns Hopkins University Press, 1963.

Nikitine, Basile. *Les Kurdes: Étude sociologique et historique.* Paris: Imprimerie Nationale, 1956.

Noel, Edward William Charles. *Diary of Major Noel on Special Duty in Kurdistan, from June 14th to September 21st, 1919.* Basra: Government Press, 1920.

Olson, Robert. *The Emergence of Kurdish Nationalism and the Sheikh Saïd Rebellion, 1880–1925.* Austin: University of Texas Press, 1989.

Petran, Tabitha. *Syria.* New York: Praeger, 1972.

Renon, Dov. *The Quest for Self-Determination.* New Haven, Conn.: Yale University Press, 1979.

Safrastian, Arshak. *Kurds and Kurdistan.* London: Arwell Press, 1948.

Seton-Watson, Hugh. *Nations and States: An Enquiry into the Origins of Nations and the Politics of Nationalism.* London: Methuen, 1977.

Sharaf al Din Khan of Bitlis. *Sharafnameh; or, Les fastes de la nation Kurdes.* Translated by F. Charmoy. St. Petersburg, 1868–76. A sixteenth-century account of the Kurdish people and their chiefs.

Silopi, Zinnar. *Doza Kurdistan.* Beirut, 1969.

Sim, Richard. *Kurdistan: The Search for Recognition.* Conflict Studies No. 124, 1980.

Smith, Anthony D. *The Ethnic Origins of Nations.* London: Basil Blackwell, 1986.

Tapper, Richard, editor. *The Conflict of Tribe and State in Iran and Afghanistan.* London: Croom-Helm, 1983.

Wahby, Tewfik. "The Origin of the Kurds and Their Language in 'Kurdistan.'" *Annual Journal of the Kurdistan Students Society in Europe.* Paris, 1965.

Xemgin, E. *Kurdistanda Insan Haklari.* Cologne: Agri Verlag, 1989.

Yildiz, Mahmut. "The Concept of Self-Determination and the Kurdish Question." Master's thesis in theory and practice of human rights, University of Essex, 1992.

Zabih, Sepehr. *The Communist Movement in Iran.* Berkeley and Los Angeles: University of California Press, 1966.